Make Money with a Microbusiness

In life, we all start small.
Why not do the same with your business ventures?

Anthony Hilb

Lift Off Publishing

Artwork by Jay Holt.

Visit my personal website at www.AnthonyHilb.com

For more resources, visit www.MicrobusinessOwners.com

Printed in the United States of America

First Printing: 2013

ISBN: 0989110508

ISBN-13: 978-0-9891105-0-1

For my lovely wife, Nichole.

A special thank you to my team.

For immediate microbusiness ideas, see Chapter 4 on page 52.

For help executing your ideas, see Chapter 6 on page 70.

If there was no such thing as money, you could still expect something in return for your products and services. Providing excellent products and services would still give you freedom if we simply practiced trade. I wrote this book to help you make money in order to buy your needs, wants, freedom, and help more people. The more people you help, the more freedom you'll have.

With advancements in technology, it's easier than ever to help more people. Make that your focus. You can help more people with more money, but money isn't everything. Our lives have so much more meaning and happiness when we connect our wants and needs with ongoing actions that truly help other people.

CONTENTS

A Few Thoughts About Microbusinesses

- Status updates with social media websites such as Twitter, Facebook, Google+, and LinkedIn are often referred to as microblogs. Microblogs are typically easier and more fun to manage than traditional blogs. The same often holds true for microbusinesses versus bigger businesses.

- "Microbusinesses aren't new; they've been around since the beginning of commerce. What's changed, however, is the ability to test, launch, and scale your project quickly and on the cheap." – Chris Guillebeau – *The $100 Startup*

- "As many as one-third of workers in the United States work independently." – Sarah Horowitz –*The Freelancer's Bible*

- Anyone who owns a business with fewer than 10 employees can be considered a microbusiness owner.

- A few examples of microbusinesses include locally owned coffee shops, barber shops, hair salons, web developers, app developers, DJs, photographers, private tutors, private music instructors, personal fitness trainers, private medical practices, small marketing and SEO firms, small law firms, small lawn care companies, local plumbing services, small heating and cooling services, as well as private consultants.

Benefits of Owning a Microbusiness

- You can pursue multiple small projects, which gives you a variety of income opportunities. Many people enjoy this more than relying on one source of income that consumes all of their time.

- You can choose to have a much more flexible schedule and can often work from your home or wherever you want.

- Many microbusiness owners work for 10 – 30 hours a week and make just as much and sometimes more than those who work 40+ hours a week at a traditional job.

- You can choose with whom you work. If you don't enjoy working with an employee or customer, you can easily go your separate ways. As an employee at a typical job, you either quit or continue to work with people you don't enjoy.

- In many cases, you won't need more than a few hundred dollars to start the beginning phases of your microbusiness.

- You can make your microbusiness your full-time job, your part-time job, or a way to make extra money in your spare time each year. It's up to you – your business, your rules.

- You don't have to deal with office politics on a daily or weekly basis. Come to think of it, you don't ever have to deal with office politics. You just need to be a good, honest person who creates a positive impact on peoples' lives with your products and services.

- You can charge rates that are fair for both yourself and your customers.

Chapter 0 – Why Microbusiness?

In life, we all start small. Why not do the same with your business ventures?

Why am I using the term 'microbusiness' instead of 'small business,' 'sole proprietorship,' 'independent contractor,' or 'freelance worker?' While the term 'small business' can also be applied to what we're calling a microbusiness, a small business can have anywhere from 1 to 500 employees, encompassing a much wider variety of organizations than we'll be discussing. As you may know, a sole proprietorship is a kind of business entity. I use the term 'microbusiness' to describe not a business entity, but a business that requires little or no debt to start while being run by a single individual or very small team.

I prefer the term 'microbusiness owner' or simply 'business owner' to the terms 'independent contractor' and 'freelance worker' because I believe it's important to be proud of your projects while also claiming your ownership of them.

Since there are many different opinions about the number of employees that constitute a microbusiness, let's keep it simple and say that number can range anywhere from 1 – 10 individuals. As a note: I will only be using the number of employees to define a microbusiness – not the annual revenue. Although this definition isn't exactly correct, this approach will help acknowledge the ever-increasing impact of a small team.

According to the Small Business Administration (SBA), the official size category of your business varies by industry. To learn more about this, visit the SBA's Guide to Size Standards.[1] If you meet the listed criteria and consider yourself a microbusiness, the type of business structure you choose is still up to you.

Why 'microbusiness' rather than 'micro business,' the hyphenated 'micro-business,' or the original 'micro-enterprise?' I've read all of these variations in different online blogs, articles, and books. Currently, The Oxford English Dictionary Online approves of 'microbusiness,' and they produce "the world's most trusted dictionaries."[2] Dictionary.com is fine with it, too.

If you have never started a business, a microbusiness is a great place to begin. You will need little money, you can do much of the work from your home, you won't need full-time employees at first (if ever), and you don't have to quit your current job. Though everyone will take on different levels of risk, keep in mind that starting extremely small with no debt is often an option. Because of this, even if you later decide to fold, the only thing you will have lost is time. As Seth Godin says, "It is so cheap to fail today compared to what it was to fail 50 years ago."[3]

In the beginning, it's usually best to have another source of income. During the test marketing period, microbusinesses are most appealing to people who have another job or are looking for another job so they won't need a living wage from the business overnight. It may also provide individuals looking for a traditional job with extra money before they find a full-time job opportunity.

Many microbusiness owners make a modest amount of money. But hey, if you lose your job or you're looking for a job, it's nice to own one so you have some source of income and possibly a creative outlet.

Then there's Instagram; they only had 13 employees when they sold their business for $1 billion to Facebook.[4] I know, I suggested we make it easy and consider a microbusiness to be a business that has 1 – 10 employees, but Instagram is close enough and definitely worth mentioning.

The point is this: With technology evolving at such an incredible speed, your chances of owning a business with a few employees that makes you an impressive sum of money, while improving many lives, are greater than ever.

Risk

You could take a less risky approach by providing a service and earn an extra $10,000 a year aside from your day job. Starting multiple microbusinesses is another option if you can manage it. Or, like most microbusiness owners, you could make a living wage from $25,000 to $100,000 annually.[5] Also possible is a larger sum of $2 million or more a year with your microbusinesses. The amount you can make varies incredibly.

The beginning stages of most microbusinesses are appealing, especially if you don't borrow any money to start your project. Remember, you can work at your own pace. You shouldn't need more than $5,000 to get started with many businesses; many times you'll only need a few hundred bucks.

I started my first microbusiness with an initial investment of $50, the old minivan my parents gave me, and a laptop. I didn't even have another source of income. Fifteen years ago, I probably would have still been working in an office. But the workforce is drastically changing, and I'm prepared to evolve with it. So I said screw it, quit everything else, and went full speed ahead with my first microbusiness!

Again, I recommend starting with another source of income in the beginning, so you don't have to worry about bills and buying groceries like I did. Although I wasn't making much money at first, my microbusiness still prevented me from moving back into my parents' place after college.

Instead of wasting my entire day applying for jobs, I advertised some of the work I was willing to perform in online classifieds, which started making me a little bit of money within a week. The opportunities didn't stop there. People started referring me to their friends, and it quickly turned into a full-time job. Fast-forward two years, and I still haven't stopped.

The money I made from those beginning work opportunities also helped convince my wife (girlfriend at the time) to move in with me! Now I make a decent amount providing help with private tutoring, private consulting, freelance writing, small home improvement projects, and my publishing company.

There are plenty of projects you can start online. You can also pick up all kinds of work on websites similar to freelancer.com, or you could sell software and a variety of other products on your website, Amazon, eBay, and other online platforms. The products you decide to sell online might catch on and make you a nice income.

BASES LOADED!

You may be a student who has time to work on a microbusiness aside from school. If you have finally cut loose from video games, you can set aside 2-3 hours a day to start your own microbusiness. However, you may need to continue playing video games, since your project could be developing a new game online that is also featured in the app store for computers, smart phones, and tablets.

A company called Mojang AB earned $90 million in 2012. They own a popular video game called Minecraft, and they only had 29 employees that year! Mojang AB brought in more than half the sum of another online gaming company called Zynga Inc. in 2012. Guess how many employees Zynga has? 3,000.[6] Zynga may do better in the coming years now that they are thinking about launching online gambling games which use real currency, but regardless, we will continue to see similar trends and the power of small when comparing companies.

It has already been established – small is the new big. Micro is up to bat with bases loaded.

If you have dreams of owning a big business that makes you rich and famous, forget owning a "startup" business. Start extremely small with very little debt and test the idea rather than hiring people right away and taking on a large amount of debt. When I say start extremely small, I mean only put a couple of hours into the business each day in the beginning aside from school, your full-time job, part-time job, or job search.

If you no longer want to continue at your current job and some of your advertisements get you plenty of work, this may be the beginning of your first successful microbusiness. When my advertisements started keeping me busy, I began to focus most of my time and energy on my microbusiness rather than looking for an employee position. I'm happy I made this decision and countless others who have made this leap are, too.

Not taking on more than $1,000 of debt would be ideal in the beginning. That way you won't have a lot of debt from a previous project that didn't work to hold you back from future endeavors. Not starting with any debt is the way to go if you're starting a service such as lawn care or private tutoring. Simply post ads in a variety of locations and on websites where people in your community will notice them. You can also take the old school route of putting flyers in stores and other places people will be able to find them. I secured a high volume of work by hanging flyers on doors in nice neighborhoods. Fortunately, I learned that I needed a solicitor's license before I got in trouble!

This is an inexpensive way to see what kind of demand there is for the work you're willing to perform. If you get a lot of work, you can grow your business at your own unique pace. Remember this quote from the incredible book *Rework:* "Don't be insecure about aiming to be a small business. Anyone who runs a business that's sustainable and profitable, whether it's big or small, should be proud."[7]

When you take the microbusiness path, you will also have complete ownership of your business. Forget equity funding if you still want your freedom. I admit this is a case-by-case scenario, but wouldn't you rather be in control of your business and prevent yourself from being fired from your own company?

I'm not against all big businesses, and I'm fully aware that many times people have to take on huge sums of debt or put in much of their own money to get their business up and running. The idea and plan of execution are that strong. Many of the most profitable companies in the world are a result of venture capital. Look at Intel, Apple, Google, Genentech, FedEx, Cisco, and many others. Sometimes there is no option other than putting yourself on the line and rolling the dice. If it's an opportunity that needs to be capitalized on NOW, equity funding isn't a bad idea as long as you still own at least 51% of your company.

More often than not, it's better to start small, build a customer base, and gradually grow your business if you want to take a more conservative route to owning a big business. By taking this approach, you'll learn very important lessons on a much less painful scale, you'll be much more agile, and you'll have so much more freedom to do whatever you want with your business. You may even decide to stick with operating on a microbusiness to small business scale rather than expanding. If you have to roll the dice and take major risks, think of Bill Gates for inspiration: "To win big, <u>sometimes</u> you have to take big risks."[8]

Many people grow their businesses for noble reasons. They want to take more responsibility and give more people good jobs. These social businesses often want to create a positive, powerful impact on the world; many times it's easier for them to do this with a bigger business. They grow their businesses not strictly for more profits, but to increase their positive influence and inspire major changes that will make this world a better place. If this is your goal, but you're new to the business world, starting with a microbusiness is still likely to be your best bet. The microbusiness approach can also work for big businesses starting a new venture or subsidiary. The key is to start small and gradually grow.

Add Value

When you own a microbusiness, you'll often be able to add value to your customers' lives by giving them a more exclusive experience than bigger businesses. Your customers will appreciate the fact that they are usually working directly with the owner.

Adding value to peoples' lives is the best way to increase your chances of success with your business ventures. If you don't do that, your chances of succeeding drop significantly. So do your best to work hard and be fair to the people with whom you choose to surround yourself.

This doesn't mean you're not allowed to make mistakes. I've done a great job for the majority of my customers, but I've also done some work that didn't go well. This was especially true in the summer of 2011 when I first started doing home maintenance work. Continuing to learn and improve has enabled me to stay successful.

You'll be able to start a microbusiness at your own convenience and grow the business however you want. If it doesn't work, you can simply move on to other projects since you didn't take on much, if any, debt to start. If the next project is successful, you can grow at a pace that is right for you while comfortably maintaining your business and personal life.

Even George Bluth from *Arrested Development* owns a microbusiness. "There's always money in the banana stand!"[9]

Embrace the Chaos!

The suggestions in this book may work for you, or they might not. Different approaches work for different people. Life is often unpredictable and each day is a gift, so you might as well embrace life's random variables and move forward with a grateful mind. That being said, I'm writing from my successful experience as a microbusiness owner. I believe my experience and research will help many of you who want to start a microbusiness.

It's my hope that this book will, at the very least, change the way you think about business and the future of business. I'd also like to sell you on starting your own microbusiness. Why not give it a shot? Again, it can be a full-time job, part-time job, or an endeavor you only pursue a few times a year. Maybe one of your microbusinesses will change the world. You'll never know if you don't go for it. You don't have to pay for access to many classifieds websites, and building relationships with people can happen faster than ever with evolving technology and social networks.

The majority of this book will discuss actions you can take to improve your business life as well as your personal life. When you're starting a microbusiness, the two go hand in hand. Even if you're an employee, unemployed with no source of income, or an owner of a big business with 7,000 employees, I still believe your personal life affects your performance in all areas.

As the owner of a microbusiness, you will often find yourself doing much of the work in your apartment, home, or garage during the first few months or years, making your personal life and business life much more intimate than many other work circumstances.

In the following pages, I will blend your business and personal life by discussing topics such as:

- Your social life
- Managing your time
- Preparation and microbusiness ideas
- Launching a brighter future
- How to get customers and keep them
- Handling your competition
- Managing your personal and business finances
- Endurance
- Staying informed

- How to have a good time through it all
- The art of giving
- More thoughts about the microbusiness revolution!

We will take a look at my personal experiences, what other successful microbusiness owners have to say about their experiences, as well as other research that show the power and potential of microbusinesses.

Change the World for the Better

Be unconventional. You don't have to do business the same way the majority of people in your line of work are doing business. As a business owner, it's your job to make constructive improvements in your chosen field or fields. You may be an outcast when you're the first person to do something drastically different, but if you're making changes that add more value to peoples' lives, your ideas will quickly stick. You could even change the world with your ideas and improvements.

Changing the world doesn't necessarily mean creating a big business that goes public. You can change the world by owning a business with two employees that provides its customers with fair deals and kindness. Your business may inspire a younger person who looks up to you to start businesses of his or her own one day too, and their businesses may make this world an even better place. You never know whom you will inspire. Remember to do your best to provide your employees, customers, friends, and family with a positive experience when you interact with them.

Your interactions with all of these people may not always be positive and uplifting. Sometimes you have to walk away from certain situations – cooperation is a two-way street. That's why your best bet is to choose with whom you spend your time extremely carefully. This is one of the most important and challenging steps you will take on the road to success. As a microbusiness owner, you can do just that by having the ability to choose both your coworkers and clients. I wish you all the success you can handle!

Chapter 1 – Your Team

"Keep away from people who try to belittle your ambitions. Small people always do that, but the really great make you feel that you, too, can become great."

–Mark Twain

I define my team as anybody I spend time with or talk with on a weekly to monthly basis. These people include family, friends, customers, and the occasional people I hire to help me with business projects. Fortunately, I have a brilliant team. I'm extremely lucky to have such a wonderful wife along with supportive friends, family members, and customers. Deciding to go separate ways with unhelpful, unsupportive individuals certainly helped me find the people I love working and spending time with today.

When you work at a bigger, traditional business, dealing with office politics will probably become a daily reality. It's difficult to cut yourself loose from people you don't get along with in this type of work circumstance. Though dealing with office politics can be a valuable skill to learn, you'll rarely have to address this when you own a microbusiness – as the owner, you will have more control over your work environment.

Some important questions to consider: Are the people you surround yourself with supporting you? Are you supporting them? There's nothing like spending time with people you truly care about who also care about you. You will accomplish your goals much faster and be inspired when you spend time with them. Those who don't respect you or care about your well-being will derail you from your goals quickly.

However, the people around you may be doing their best to build you up and take you to great heights. Make sure you are not your own worst enemy or a negative person in somebody else's life.

Feedback is often misinterpreted as being unsupportive. Many times people who are actually supportive come off as unsupportive when they are giving you their opinions. Occasionally, they may resort to harshly criticizing you in an effort to save you from a course of action with which they completely disagree.

You need feedback to make both yourself and your business better. Remind yourself and others around you that constructive criticism means exercising helpful advice without being harsh and disrespectful. Also remember that criticism can often be avoided altogether. Rather than telling someone how 'wrong' they are, ask them questions and learn why they think the way they do. Or ask how they feel about taking a different course of action. You can also point them in a different direction without criticizing them.

If you have an excellent employee but disagree with their plan of action, let them make the potential mistake if the consequences won't be too severe.

Think about the mistakes open-source organizations like *Wikipedia* and Android endure. Yet so many of us rely on *Wikipedia* and Android devices every day.

Look for supportive and helpful qualities in family, friends, co-workers, employees, customers, and anyone else you will spend time with on a weekly or monthly basis. Remember to encourage those around you even if their projects aren't going well; improvements can be made!

Cutting yourself loose from people who don't support and respect you may be painful in the moment, but you won't regret it. In fact, you'll probably experience the opposite of regret when you think back to how you didn't stick around. And forget about holding grudges. "Being angry and resentful of someone is like letting them live rent-free in your head."[1] -George Foreman

→→Move Forward →→

When you are surrounded with supportive individuals, you will experience better opportunities and much healthier relationships. The importance of your team cannot be overlooked!

Growing?

Consider the power of crowdsourcing and crowd funding before hiring full-time employees. Crowdsourcing and crowd funding are currently key components to changing the world with a microbusiness. You can post any size project that you need help with on countless websites – and the number of websites on which you can post projects is growing. I posted one of my projects on the popular website reddit.com and it was completed within 24 hours! I paid the artist using PayPal.

If you hire full-time employees, remember the wisdom of Richard Branson, the founder and chairman of Virgin Group:

"Find good people - set them free."[2]

"Employees are number one. The way you treat your employees is the way they will treat your customers."[3]

According to Branson, the 'Virgin type' of person is all over the world. He says, "These people, by their nature and their outlook on life, enjoy working with others. They're attentive. They smile freely. They're often lively and fun to be with."[2]

One last quote by Branson...it's one of my favorites:

"Ethics aren't just important in business. They are the whole point of business."[4]

When you hire people with integrity, great attitudes, high energy, and drive, you get outstanding results and your employees get freedom.

Notice how one of Richard Branson's top priorities is finding good people and letting them learn from their own mistakes. Branson understands the importance of his team and that knowledge has served him well!

Chapter 2 – Flying Time

"An ounce of action is worth a ton of theory."

–Ralph Waldo Emerson

Many full-time microbusiness owners can't afford to waste time. These are the business owners who get paid an hourly rate or have to be at a certain place at a certain time. There are, however, a number of exceptions. One instance in which this rule doesn't apply involves those individuals who earn residual incomes. A residual income is money you receive for an initial effort that requires less work in the future. Some residual income opportunities can include:

- Owning storage units and collecting rent from them.
- Owning a house or apartments and charging people rent.
- Owning vending machines.
- Owning ATM machines.
- Owning a restaurant or other type of business that has enough success to hire a manager responsible for all of the hiring and supervising.
- Blogging and building content rich websites.

- Developing applications for computers, smart phones, and tablets.

Countless employees get paid vacations, and sometimes they get more job security than being a business owner. Nice isn't it? Here's the catch: When you own a microbusiness, you will often be able to perform your work anywhere, even when you're on vacation.

We're all pressured to get jobs and pay our bills. It's understandable, and it can be fun when you don't simply focus on just making enough money to pay for your basic needs. It's more fun when you have exciting financial goals because you have a much better reason to get up in the morning. That doesn't mean you should instantly set yourself up with far-fetched financial goals. But an extra $5,000 - $10,000 this year would be nice, wouldn't it? Many people have jobs they enjoy, and they don't feel as though they are wasting any time.

I recently asked my dad how he has felt about his 30-year career with his company, and he said he has loved it. He said there were many challenges, but in the end, it has always been worth it. He said he has liked the security, the people with whom he works, the regular hours, the pension, and the insurance. Both he and my mom have been such an inspiration to me.

Bottom line? Not everybody wants to own a business, and being an employee can definitely be a rewarding experience (though the 30-year career path has become much less common). Being an employee can be very fun and logical. I took an employee position after I graduated from college, and it was an amazing experience. My boss knew exactly how to work with me, and each day was productive. I would have stayed for the long-term, but the company was going out of business.

Conversely, many people have jobs they don't like that range from low paying to high paying. I've been reading business books since I was a kid that underscore how important our time is, yet many of us often don't consider its true value.

For the people who don't have specialized skill sets or solid career paths, it's usually easier to look for new opportunities or start a business. For the people with specialized skill sets and careers, it feels riskier to start something new. I can't blame many of these people for sticking with their jobs. However, let's not overlook the disadvantages of only having one time-consuming primary source of income while dealing with difficult office politics.

When office politics become a serious problem as an employee and reasoning with those around you doesn't work, we either walk or stay put. It's not a bad idea to stay and do your job. You'll get experience, you'll get better at cooperating, and as a result, you may have solid job security with good pay.

When the company I just mentioned was going out of business, I found a different job that wasn't worth my time. The office politics were pointless. The owner understood why I wanted to leave, and we're still on good terms. I didn't like quitting on him, but I was starting to experience success with my first microbusiness, and I knew that was what I really wanted to pursue.

I knew that day I was making a very important life decision. The paths were crystal clear: I could continue to endure pointless office theatrics and be a pushover, or I could take a stand and do things my own way and create my own multiple sources of income. The result? I'm much happier on my own and already make more than I was making at that job. I no longer have one source of income taking up the majority of my workday – I have multiple small sources of income that add up to a nice amount. It has been much more secure than relying on one paycheck.

Divide Your Time and Conquer!

Be sure to diversify your income opportunities. This will give you more security. A successful product or subscription service is ideal for building a variety of customers, but this example also applies to traditional service businesses. Example: If you own a local marketing company, take on multiple clients who all agree that you'll perform five hours of work a week for $75. You could also agree to a weekly set of tasks that will not take more than five hours of your time per client. This will enable you to have ten clients making you $750 a week for 50 hours of work. You may even be able to charge $20 an hour, making you $1,000 a week before taxes from those ten clients.

If you're doing excellent work for all of your clients, you probably won't lose all of them, and it's very unlikely that you will lose all ten of them in one week. This is a major reason I like owning a business. Many times, working a traditional job involves having only one source of income. This is similar to starting a business and having only one client that consumes 40 hours of your time each week. You abruptly lose all of your weekly income if you lose that client. Unemployment is set up for traditional workers in the event they lose their jobs, but it's rather depressing.

If you do have a traditional 9-5, owning a microbusiness on the side can be a great solution. If you lose your job, you'll have some source of income, and you may not need to rely on money from unemployment. You'll also feel good about having other work opportunities while looking for another job, and maybe you'll get enough work from your microbusiness to take the leap and make it a full-time project!

In his book *The $100 Startup,* Chris Guillebeau says, "The microbusiness revolution is happening all around us as people say 'thanks, but no thanks' to traditional work, choosing to chart their own course and create their own future."[1]

Check out Chris Guillebeau's books if you haven't already. His valuable book *The Art of Non-Conformity* inspired me to donate profits from this book to charity: water. Thanks, Chris!

If you don't want to start a business, exciting jobs are out there. You may have to relocate or take a few years off to learn new skills. Or you may have to spend three to five years looking for opportunities while working jobs you don't enjoy very much. Rewarding jobs exist, and you shouldn't stop looking if you don't already have one. They aren't necessarily in a particular field; they could be in any field. It's really all about keeping a good attitude, the people you're working with, your skill sets, and your creativity.

Just remember this if you have trouble finding work right away: There's always somebody, somewhere, who needs help with something. Think of things people need help with, where they are, and then go out there and provide those practical products and services! You may have to learn new skills, so hurry up and get started!

Highlights

- Your time is valuable.
- Divide your time and conquer!
- Fun jobs exist.
- You can start a business and create a nice place to work – where people work together rather than against each other.

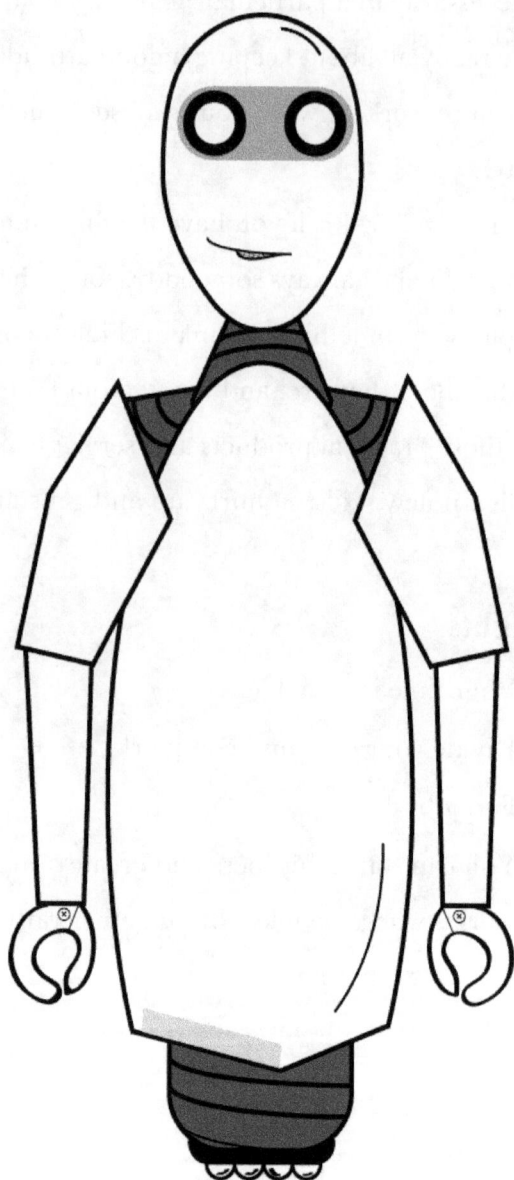

Chapter 3

A Lesson in Overextending Yourself

Overextending yourself can lead to mediocrity on all levels.

You may want to be excellent at everything. If you're attending college full-time, working a full-time job, maintaining a social life, and starting a business, your chances of a mediocre performance in all areas will greatly increase.

Pulling it all off can be impressive, but at what cost? I no longer believe 'pulling it off' is good enough. I used to think that doing a passable job with as many projects as possible was fine. This is no longer the case. Today, I ruthlessly prioritize my time.

The key is to find your own unique balance. If you're great at multi-tasking many projects, go for it. If you're like me and prioritizing your projects is a better fit, that's fine too. As I just mentioned in the previous chapter, it's important to have multiple customers for diverse income opportunities, but be sure you don't overextend yourself to the point that you are not providing quality work for your customers.

Do the Math and Reinvent Your ρ∀Th

Thinking of your life as a business is helpful. If you like money, this method makes perfect sense. Although life isn't all about money, it happens to be what currently gives us freedom in this world. Figure out how much time you are approximately going to spend on a project or hobby and do the math to learn how much money you'll make within that time frame.

I realized I was spending at least 25-30 hours a week playing drums and studying music. After getting real with myself and doing the math, I learned I wasn't making much money at all. This isn't true for plenty of performing musicians out there, but it is often enough.

This is where creativity and reinventing your path come into play. Creativity is the answer. Creativity is what invents new paths. As Jason Fried and David Heinemeier Hansson say:

"What distinguishes people who are ten times more effective from the norm is not that they work ten times as hard; it's that they use their creativity to come up with solutions that require one-tenth of the effort."[1] *Rework*

I was performing live shows at different venues on the weekends – something countless musicians do. I was doing it because I love music. But what if I had also decided to build a blog, website, YouTube channel, and app around my passion for drums way back in 2007? I could have taken it even further and thought of many more original, creative ways to connect with people through music online.

This could have enabled me to promote my blog and YouTube channel for hours every day while sharing educational videos, sheet music, and news articles about playing drums with a potential large audience on the internet. A few banner ads and a decent amount of traffic could have turned that lower income into a higher figure – maybe an additional 10k or more a year. Worst-case scenario: even if it didn't translate into an income, it could have all been done from the comfort of my home as a part-time endeavor for a small time and money investment.

Evolving with technology while thinking of creative ways to share your passions is the key here. Always ask, "How can I creatively share my passions with people?" Sharing your passions and products on the internet obviously connects you to far more people than only selling your products and services locally.

The local store that sells their products in person, on eBay, Amazon, Etsy, and other websites will outperform the store that doesn't utilize the internet. This isn't new, but there is still a huge market for sharing information, products, services, and your passions with people online. The market might get too saturated within the next few years, but currently there are still major opportunities online. Take advantage of them!

Although I love music and still play drums, I realized I was much more passionate about business and pursuing work that directly helps other people. But that's just me; you have to prioritize what's right for you — just remember to do the math and reinvent your path!

On a side note: Listening to music that inspires you can often help you with your creative breakthroughs.

Avoid Loans Until You Have Success

The financial aspects of overextension can be very sad. Taking out a loan for a product or service that has not been tested is usually unnecessary, and it can easily lead to bankruptcy. If you've experienced this, don't lose hope; read the article *7 Wildly Successful People Who Survived Bankruptcy*.[2]

The key is to make sure your business has steady customers before you expand. Even Facebook had plenty of promise and users before they took on major debt. Mark Zuckerberg launched 'Thefacebook' on February 4th, 2004, and in just three weeks it had 6,000 users. When Facebook was exclusively available to Harvard, Columbia, Stanford, and Yale, it was only costing Zuckerberg $85 a month for server space.[3]

Fast-forward to the end of the summer in 2004, and Facebook had about 200,000 users.[4] This huge increase in users also resulted in an increased cost of business operations. Mark Zuckerberg and his family spent around $85,000 from their own pockets on Facebook during the summer of 2004 to keep up with the costs.[5] It was at this point when Facebook took on an outside loan of $500,000 from Peter Thiel, the co-founder of PayPal.[6] Remember: many times you won't need to take on major outside loans until after you have plenty of customers and promise.

My former business advisor encouraged me to take out a $50,000 loan for my business early in 2012. That was when I only had a few customers, so I obviously didn't take on that kind of debt. I believe it's smarter to start extremely small and experience firsthand what the demand is for a project. If the demand for my work dramatically increases,

I may take on a small amount of debt in relation to what I'm making each year. I would take on a small amount of debt at that point because my idea will be tested, I will have a better understanding of what the demand is for my business, and I'll have even more customers. Again, it will be a small amount in relation to how much the business profits, which will make it easier to pay off if I want to fold the business and focus on different opportunities.

A Steady Pace Wins the Race!

If you have to turn many customers down, scale back on your advertisements for the time being. It will harm you more in the long run if you can't keep up with the demands of your customers. Keep a steady pace and increase your marketing efforts as you increase the amount of time, employees, products, and services you have to offer. Unsatisfied customers can be the worst form of marketing. Keep your customers happy and they will say good things about you, allowing you to stay in business.

Not pushing yourself to improve your business because of the fear of financially overextending yourself can be damaging. You may miss out on opportunities that could have led to an amazing future and terrific financial gains. But if you do miss out on those opportunities, you still won't have debt. You will simply have missed opportunities. If you financially overextend yourself, you will have debt in anticipation of customers. When you analyze it, financially overextending yourself can be more detrimental than starting your business at a micro level and slowly growing. If you overextend yourself and fail, you may have serious debt holding you back from future projects.

Give 100% to your prioritized projects each day. Focusing your energy on school and your microbusiness during the day can usually be balanced while maintaining great performances.

There are instances when financially overextending yourself pays off tremendously. Guys like Bill Gates, Mark Zuckerberg, and Steve Jobs took big financial risks, and they reaped huge rewards. However, they prioritized their projects and quit school. They did the math and realized they either needed to drop out of college or make business a top priority. We all know their time management and math skills paid off!

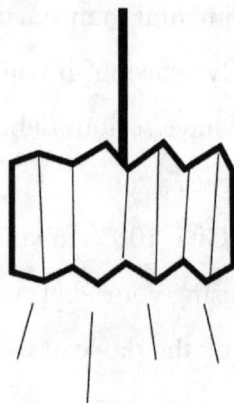

Chapter 4 – The Will to Prepare

"By failing to prepare, you are preparing to fail."

–Benjamin Franklin

Surrounding ourselves with uplifting people, setting attainable goals, and keeping an eye on our valuable time are three factors that cannot have their significance underlined enough. All of these key aspects are improved by laying a foundation of thorough preparation. Constantly reading and researching is a great place to begin. This simple change has far reaching effects in both your personal and business life.

Proper preparation requires gaining a variety of skills and knowledge. The top achievers are lifelong learners. They continuously study a variety of books, learn new skills, and sharpen their knowledge. I recently assigned Max Park, a seventh grade student I'm tutoring, a paper about the importance of learning. Here's one sentence from his paper with which I strongly agree: "Learning has a significant place in life and will continue to maintain that position."

I'm currently reading *The Mackay MBA of Selling in the Real World* by Harvey Mackay. This book is full of sagacious tips from Mackay. At 81 years old, he has accrued plenty of wisdom to share.

Mackay's book also highlights how much effort he has invested to achieve success. While reading is extremely important, make no mistake: There are certain things you can only learn from hard work and experience. When you study the most successful people in the world, you will certainly find at least one common denominator: drive.

As Harvey Mackay says, "Desire isn't enough. You must have the will to prepare. Preparation means yearning, learning, reading, listening, organizing, and expanding your thinking. It involves rigorous training of your mind and body to achieve success."[1]

Asking better questions will help you dramatically when you're preparing for a project or a long-term goal. Here are some questions to consider:

- What value are you actually adding to peoples' lives?
- How are you making a positive difference?
- What changes do you need to make in order to best meet the needs of your customers?
- How can you get more customers?
- How can you be the best at what you do?
- Why? Why not?

All the marketing in the world won't help you if you're not frequently striving to improve by thinking about questions like these.

One remark I like to keep in mind on this topic is from Tony Robbins: "Quality questions create a quality life. Successful people ask better questions, and as a result, they get better answers."

Set Your Goals

Set goals you'd like to accomplish this week, this month, this year, five years from now, ten years from now, and within your lifetime. Constantly review and fantasize about them. A few categories you may want to include are: personal, family, health, financial, business, charity, and travel. Reminding yourself of these goals will help keep you motivated and on the right path.

A Few Microbusiness Ideas

Being prepared includes having a list of ideas that you are willing to experiment with when it comes to your microbusiness ventures. This step can often be challenging, so I've put a list of examples together for you.

Important: Make sure you are not violating any of the contracts you signed with your current employer or any previous employers. If you're not stealing anything from these organizations, but you still want to stay in the same field with your microbusiness, your current and past employers may agree to sign a contract that supersedes any previous agreements. Be sure to check with them before going forward.

Also make sure you're legally operating your microbusiness ventures. Pay your taxes properly and set up the right business insurance if it's a requirement. During the very early days of operating, it's usually okay to perform many of the jobs listed in the following pages without working out every detail, but I can't make any guarantees. If your microbusiness becomes a full-time job, be sure you're legal in all areas. Seeking help from professionals is a good idea at this point.

There is much grey area and flexibility in your pursuit of work, but let's keep it extremely simple and break it down into two categories:

1. Learn a skill that most people don't have the time or patience to acquire. Ideally, you will be able to learn skills that don't require a lot of money or a college degree. However, doctors, professors, lawyers, accountants, public school teachers, engineers, scientists, and many other professionals that need certification to operate also fit in this category.

2. Start a business based around work that many people aren't willing to perform. Examples include trash removal, physical labor, construction, plumbing, and many others.

Remember: "The laws of supply and demand apply not only to commodities but to the choices people make."[2]

Let's start with the first category of microbusiness ideas:

- Invent. Learn how to code. Create new software. Learn how to patent, trademark, and execute your ideas. Think of your own creative microbusiness ideas that will make peoples' lives better. Pay attention to 3D printing and read *Makers* by Chris Anderson.

- Learn how to develop applications for computers, smart phones, and tablets. Learn how to develop applications within Facebook, WordPress, and other websites.

- Continue to learn how to help people with new technology and earn money with those skills.

- Become an expert in math, chemistry, English, and other often challenging subjects. Offer private tutoring services.

- Use your English skills to offer editorial work, content management, and other writing assistance.

- Start a niche blog and website. With this option, especially, age is not a limiting factor. Still in middle school or high school? The microbusiness you start may positively transform your life. That's what happened to Emerson Spartz. He created the #1 Harry Potter website in the world (mugglenet.com) at age 12, personally met J.K. Rowling, and he still graduated from the University of Notre Dame. After graduating, he expanded and is now the CEO of Spartz Media (spartzmedia.com). They have had as many as 160 million page views a month!

- Learn and understand the importance of graphic design. Dylan Spartz has been designing with Spartz Media since he was only 13 years old. He has been building some of the most popular websites on the internet with his brother and the Spartz Media team for over 10 years!

- Earn money playing poker online and offline. It's not for everyone, and it's definitely a skill that takes time, but my close friends Ben and Brett have been doing this for years!

- Become a private consultant in your area of expertise.

- Browse sites similar to freelancer.com and craigslist for online opportunities.

- Great at social media? Start a social media management service for other businesses and individuals near and far.

- Have an eye for fashion? Buy used clothes and resell them at a higher margin online and offline.

- Buy popular items at wholesale prices and sell them on eBay, Amazon, Etsy, and other sites. Nothing new here, but it still works.

- Become a personal chef. Don't eat all of the food and watch out for food allergies!

- Have valuable experience and knowledge? Write a book and share it with the world! Physical books may not be as popular today, but so many people have smart phones and tablets. Kindle also has a free app you can download on your computer. eBooks will stick around for some time...they may even evolve into something more interactive. They already have inbound links and creative designs.

- Become a photographer. Weddings, senior photos, baby photos, seasonal photos, and family photos are just the beginning of the opportunities you'll find.

- Artistic? Offer those skills to others for reasonable rates. I love Jay Holt's artwork, so I happily hired him to help with this book!

- Not an alcoholic? Love beer? Start a microbrewery!

- Love music? Become a DJ, design music applications, start a YouTube music channel, share music news online, play in a band, make a funny music YouTube channel dedicated to skits similar to the "Harlem Shake" with your friends, and consider the long list of other music related opportunities.

You get the idea. Let's move on to the second category.

- House cleaning
- Lawn care
- Landscaping
- Home renovation
- Construction
- Car mechanic
- House painting
- Power washing
- Car washing & detailing
- Cleaning out crawl spaces
- Small scale moving service
- Barber shop or hair salon
- Furniture delivery
- Event planning
- Elderly care
- Provide a childcare service – see childcare.net for helpful advice.
- Become a nanny or manny
- Pet sitting / dog walking
- Pest control
- Locksmith

Continue to think of microbusiness ideas of your own in addition to researching the variety of opportunities listed here. Learn about the websites on which you can advertise your microbusiness ideas and continuously look for new advertising websites, apps, and other avenues.

Read *555 Ways to Earn Extra Money* by Jay Conrad Levinson (written in the 90's but it still works wonders if you make adjustments for modern technology). Also check out *101 Weird Ways to Make Money* by Steve Gillman. Be sure to keep an eye out for new books, websites, applications, and articles with creative resources for different business ideas.

By putting together a comprehensive list of tasks you are willing to perform, you prevent potential panic in the future. If times are lean and your preferred skill set is not as profitable, you can look to your pre-established list of ideas for inspiration.

Lift Off!

Chapter 5 – Launch a Brighter Future!

"Inventing is a lot like surfing: you have to anticipate and catch the wave at just the right moment."

–*Ray Kurzweil*

It's important to consider the future before you start your microbusiness.

The rate at which changes and advancements in technology are occurring is unbelievable. That's why I personally like to stick with owning microbusinesses – it enables me to adapt quickly and perform a variety of jobs.

It is important to study futurists in business even if their predictions aren't accurate. Consistently thinking about future inventions and possibilities trains you to anticipate and accept change, therefore making it easier to adapt in the business world when inevitable changes occur.

Ray Kurzweil is one of the most important futurists to study. Although some of his predictions may seem outlandish, he has established a track record of success over the past 30 years. Do yourself a favor – read Kurzweil's books and visit some of his sites to learn more:

Kurzweilai.net   Bigthink.com/raykurzweil

Transcendentman.com   Singularity.com

Abundance by Peter Diamandis and Steven Kotler is another excellent book about a positive future. To borrow their summary, it is about how "progress in artificial intelligence, robotics, infinite computing, ubiquitous broadband networks, digital manufacturing, nanomaterials, synthetic biology, and many other exponentially growing technologies will enable us to make greater gains in the next two decades than we have in the previous 200 years."[1]

Further, the progress taking place from 2032-2042 will outperform the technological gains we will achieve within the next 20 years. We've already been seeing a similar pattern. As Jeffrey Rayport points out, "The average smart phone is as powerful as a high-end Mac or PC of less than a decade ago."[2] Having a fundamental understanding of exponential growth also helps when analyzing these changes.

Technology subject to Moore's law will continue to evolve at incredible speeds. As further improvements are made with technology, prices will drop significantly, increasing accessibility to the most impoverished parts of the world.

Although many people refer to the most impoverished people in the world as the 'bottom billion,' Diamandis and Kotler choose to refer to them as 'the rising billion.' Diamandis says, "The creation of a global transportation network was the initial step down this path, but it's the combination of the Internet, microfinance, and wireless communication technology that's transforming the poorest of the poor into an emerging market force."[3]

With increasing access to inexpensive, advanced technology, it's far easier for the rising billion to make global changes. It will only become easier for this group in the future.

We are surrounded by bad news in the media. Bad news sells, and as a result, some of us often believe there isn't hope in the world. Diamandis and Kotler attest this is our greatest challenge to achieving abundance, stating: "The inability of people to see the positive trends through the sea of bad news – that may be the biggest stumbling block on the road toward abundance."[4]

More positive stories could be published than negative stories. It's not breaking news when good things are happening around the world because they are usually ordinary. This isn't a bad thing. If it were breaking news every time a plane landed safely, we would be in trouble.

See Chapter 12 for some resources to help keep your spirits up in the face of negativity.

With these exponential technologies, an abundant future for Earth is a likely possibility. Like Diamandis and Kotler state, "When seen through the lens of technology, few resources are truly scarce; they're mainly inaccessible."[5] Many people will be resistant to future breakthroughs, which isn't unusual. "People will resist breakthrough ideas until the moment they're accepted as the new norm."[6]

If you never shoot, you'll never make it.

Chapter 6 – Execution

"Ideas don't make you rich. The correct execution of ideas does."

–Felix Dennis

Test market your ideas before you make any major decisions!

If your ideas are well received during your test marketing campaign, go make some money as a sole proprietor in the beginning. Taxes are easier as a sole proprietor. As your business grows, you'll quickly be able to change your business structure to the popular limited liability company (LLC) or one of the many other business structures from which you can choose.

At this point, you will probably want to consider hiring a lawyer, accountant, and banker – an "acquisition team." They will help you with important issues such as taxes, proper licenses, business insurance, more taxes, trademarks, patents, and much more.

I recommend reading *Start Your Own Business* by the staff of Entrepreneur Media. In the most recent 2010 edition, Chapter 9 discusses the details of different business structures – sole proprietorship, partnership, corporation, limited liability company (LLC), nonprofit, and others. This is a great resource to help make an informed decision about the most fitting legal structure for your business.

Chapter 11 in *Start Your Own Business* goes into an in-depth analysis of the importance of hiring an accountant and a lawyer. "It's hard to navigate the maze of tax and legal issues facing entrepreneurs these days unless these professionals are an integral part of your team."[1]

Schedule meetings with multiple accountants and lawyers and carefully consider whom to hire. This can't be overlooked, especially if you decide to continually grow your business and increase your customer base.

To learn basic legal and accounting practices prior to hiring professionals, visit Nolo.com for helpful books and articles. Check your library for their books if you don't want to purchase them. Also consider contacting the Small Business Administration (SBA). You can send them an email at answerdesk@sba.gov or call (800) U-ASK-SBA for advice. They're open Monday – Friday from 9A.M. to 5P.M. EST. Visit them at SBA.gov. As a government-funded program, the SBA was created specifically to help people like you by answering questions and providing other beneficial (and free) resources.

You will have access to plenty of free resources to help you on your microbusiness path, but health insurance is not currently one of them (if you're operating in the U.S.). In fact, this is what stops many people from beginning their own businesses.

In many cases, people will have a part-time or full-time job that offers health benefits while also operating their own business. This can be a practical approach when you're first starting in the business world. You may work hard, get lucky, and make a nice amount of money with your microbusiness. In this case, as long as you manage your finances properly, health insurance won't be as much of a burden.

As you probably know, new health care changes enable young adults to stay on their parents' health care plan up to the age of 26. Being on your spouse's plan is also a possibility.

If none of the prior options work for you, it may be too expensive to purchase a plan for yourself and your family when you first begin. Consider registering for a group rate through your local Chamber of Commerce or the Freelancers Insurance Company (FIC). Social entrepreneur Sara Horowitz, a renowned advocate for freelance workers' rights, founded Freelancers Union and FIC. Currently, FIC is primarily available in New York state.

If you were laid off from your previous job, keep your COBRA insurance for as long as possible if the payments are within your budget. Another option is to open a high-deductible policy coupled with an HSA.

Now that we have a very basic understanding of taxes, legal matters, and insurance, we can get back to tackling your projects!

If you're starting a service-based business, post ads everywhere and call potential clients every day. If few people choose to hire your business but you still believe in it, post these same ads in different cities and on more websites. Call even more people. Some ideas may take time to become a success. Stick with them if you really believe they have potential. If you're looking for work right away, keep posting ads and making calls for different service ideas until you find some jobs.

If you're planning to launch a website, app, invention, or any other idea/product, test marketing can easily be executed.

First, make sure you have everything in order as far as copyrights, trademarks, patents, and any other legal matters go. Utilize your Facebook, Twitter, blog, reddit and other online tools and apps to help understand how well people will receive your ideas.

These online tools and applications will become more prevalent, so be sure to keep up with changes. I test marketed a picture on reddit that had a great showing – it received 35,000 views in one week![2] It didn't receive even close to this many likes on Facebook. Remember to test market your ideas and products with a variety of websites and apps at different times.

You can start extremely small and gradually grow with many business ventures. Some other endeavors will require significant amounts of startup capital. Unfortunately, I meet too many people in the business world that want to raise millions of dollars to fund their ideas. They want a big business, and they want it within the next year or two. It's as if starting small isn't even an option.

Of course, there are plenty of situations and opportunities that require you to take immediate action with a significant amount of loans and risks. However, test marketing your ideas before taking these kinds of risks is becoming so much easier. You can begin your business as a one-person operation and start offering your services this month if you don't decide to go beg for capital.

Another thing to keep in mind are the intentions of the people or businesses loaning you large sums of money.

Even Mark Cuban, who is a venture capitalist himself, advises to avoid taking on debt – especially from venture capitalists. It's pretty funny that he believes this, considering his role on the popular TV show *Shark Tank.* But I bet Cuban is an exception to this rule and better than many of the VCs out there. I would probably accept his help if he offered to finance one of my microbusinesses.

Cuban also says that he founded his first business, MicroSolutions, with an advance of $500 from his first customer. Further, he said the business had fewer than five employees and didn't grow quickly during the first couple years.

The consensus?
"It's okay to start slow. It's okay to grow slow."[3]

"The reality is that for most businesses, they don't need more cash, they need more brains."[4]

–Mark Cuban

If billionaire Mark Cuban believes this, I'm sure testing this approach won't hurt. And hey, if your business doesn't work, you won't owe anyone much money. If it does work, you can slowly grow and take on small amounts of debt in relation to what you're making.

If you still insist on raising money for your idea, ask your close friends and family and check out crowd funding websites. There are new sites like these continuously being launched, so be attentive. I haven't used any of them, but here are a few that I have found:

- Kickstarter.com
- Rockethub.com
- Indiegogo.com
- Crowdrise.com
- Have a great idea for an app? Test market it and get funding through Appbackr.com

Growing but not quite ready to hire full-time employees? Crowdsourcing is something you may want to consider if your project involves work online. As you may know, it's simply the act of outsourcing your work to people on the internet all over the world. As a freelance worker, this may also be how you find many of your work opportunities.

Making your business an open source project is another possible method of execution. *Wikipedia* and Android are examples.

Get out there and start extremely small; it should help give you an idea how interested people are in your products and services. Remember to test market and learn by visiting different websites and apps. Here are a few that may help you:

- Freelancer.com
- Craigslist
- Etsy.com
- Shopify.com
- Sell on eBay and Amazon
- Elance.com
- Twitter
- Facebook
- LinkedIn
- Google+
- Hootsuite.com
- Mashable.com
- Squidoo.com
- Infoarmy.com

- reddit.com

- Alltop.com

- Ted.com/talks

- Bigthink.com

- Microbusinessowners.com (shameless self promotion)

- Thesolopreneurlife.com

- Wearemicro.com

- Meetup.com

- Mturk.com

- Need a website? Build one quickly using wordpress.com or wordpress.org

- These online articles may also be helpful – *27 Microbusiness Tools You Didn't Know You Needed*[5] and *30 Best Sites to Find Freelance Jobs.*[6]

This is by no means a complete list of resources and tools for your microbusinesses. Always be on the look out for other helpful sites, apps, books, and more!

Chapter 7 – Competition

Do your best work.

The big fish doesn't always eat the little fish in business. Look at what happened to Kodak: they were eaten alive by a team of small fish. Online photo sharing, the digital camera technology which *they* invented, together with smart phones overtook Kodak. At Kodak's peak, these smaller businesses didn't seem to be a threat to them. But, shortly after Kodak filed for bankruptcy, Facebook was purchasing the online photo sharing company Instagram for $1 billion.[1] Other examples?

- Blockbuster versus Netflix
- Borders versus Amazon
- Medium-sized storefronts versus eBay
- Hollywood versus YouTube

As you know, Borders went out of business and Blockbuster isn't what it once was. Now medium-sized storefronts sell their inventory on eBay, and Hollywood depends on YouTube to help promote their films.

LOOK OUT! – Small fish can build a huge community and overtake the bigger fish!

We're all too familiar with competition. Competition takes place just about everywhere, and surrounds us every day. It can take place in school, at work, at home, when we're playing recreational sports, or just about any other game. Most of all, it takes place when we're competing for our survival.

In business, worrying too much about the competition can often do more harm than good. If you're just focusing on how to outperform the competition, you're giving yourself limitations while also giving the competition the lead. It is so much better to be aware of what the businesses around you are doing but to primarily focus on creating your own exceptional solutions for customers.

Competition can actually be fun. When you develop smart business tactics and operate as a microbusiness, you will be able to adapt much faster and easier than the bigger businesses around you. This agility gives you the upper hand.

The key is simple: Do your best work. Competing with yourself works to an extent, but it often gets more challenging with age. You may not be able to beat the marathon time you ran at 25 years old when you're 64. Instead, compete with yourself from a few years back or simply do the best work you can do.

If you're strictly competing with another business, you'll be satisfied as soon as you're outperforming them. This will hold you back from improvements as long as you're in the lead. This can add up to a lot of missed opportunities you would have noticed had you been doing your best work.

Be aware of your competition, but don't let them bother you too much. Above all, enjoy the day-to-day operations of your business.

Know When to Talk

While it's okay to talk about what you do, you don't have to give people every detail about your business. If you own a construction business, you wouldn't give another local construction company the names and numbers of all your clients, would you? If you were working on an invention, you wouldn't give every single detail to a competing inventor before you owned the patent and released the product.

Although I believe being generous with your information is important, it's often best to keep key information to yourself until after you've launched. I know starting a new business is exciting. You probably want to tell everybody about your new ideas, but it's smart business to keep your ideas to yourself *in the beginning* with certain endeavors.

Once you have developed a brand, it's not as big of a deal. Many people will know about your business if you market it correctly. That's the goal, isn't it? And hey, search engines, websites, apps, books, YouTube channels, documentaries, and other media have experienced massive success because of their generosity with information.

The reason I suggest keeping your ideas to yourself in the beginning is to decrease the amount of unnecessary competition you will encounter before you launch. You can avoid plenty of competition with this approach. You get the idea, and I'm sure you've heard this example many times.

If someone you know does go into a similar field, what is the solution? When you get booked, send customers their way. Hopefully they return the favor and you can work together. I exercise this approach with other contractors in my town for my home maintenance business. I'm not interested in every area of home maintenance and neither are many of the contract companies in my area. Because we all prefer to specialize, we refer each other because we trust the other will do a great job. It strengthens our brands and makes both teams better. Be sure to refer other quality, trustworthy businesses.

Sooner or later, you will inspire competition. Your business will be off the ground, and you'll have such a positive reputation that you'll be able to compete as long as you continue to evolve and do your best work.

This brings us to the choice of your fields if you haven't decided on any yet, or if you're looking for other avenues. I used part of this Felix Dennis quote in Chapter 4 before discussing a variety of microbusiness ideas; the rest of it applies here very well: "Forget glamour if the getting of money is your priority. The laws of supply and demand apply not only to commodities but to the choices people make. Too many people wish to make blockbuster movies and live in Beverly Hills."[2]

If you really need work right away, search for jobs people don't want to perform. It may not be glamorous, but you'll make money. Trash removal and lawn care are two examples.

Dennis is honest about the nature of the business world. His input equips young entrepreneurs, small business owners, microbusiness owners, and potential business owners with invaluable knowledge, providing a strong foundation.

Chapter 8 – Managing Your Finances

"There are only two reasonable sources of capital for startup entrepreneurs: your own pocket and your customers' pockets."

–Mark Cuban

Although you probably practice many of these actions, I learned some of these tips the hard way, so I wanted to share them with you:

- Identify your wants and needs.

- Develop multiple streams of income.

- Buy your food at grocery stores offering competitive rates while cutting back on going out to eat.

- Buy your clothes from places like Plato's Closet, Goodwill, and the variety of other used clothing stores. Don't like used clothes? No problem. Look at discount stores similar to T.J. Maxx.

- Rent books, DVDs, and music from the library rather than buying them.

- Need a car? Buy used. Be sure to get it checked by a reliable mechanic before you purchase it. Even Sam Walton drove a beat up truck.

- Need to redecorate your apartment or house? Again, visit Goodwill, Salvation Army, or other second hand stores instead of high price retailers. You won't feel too bad when you never use those miscellaneous items you bought, because they will probably cost $5 - $50 total, unlike the $50 - $500 you would have spent at many other stores. You can save a lot of extra money when you develop this habit.

- Buy used/passable equipment for your business in the beginning - you can buy better equipment as your customers and profits increase.

- Buy only what you need for your business. Ideally, it should be something that will be used repeatedly. It wouldn't make sense to buy an expensive piece of equipment if you won't need to use it regularly. If you need a product for a special job, stick with renting it as long as the renters are asking a reasonable price.

- If possible, only reinvest a *portion* of your profits back into your businesses.

- Study books about finance. Want to make long-term investments? Consider index funds. Vanguard is a reputable company to help you manage this.

- Learn basic accounting.

- Do the math!

Chapter 9 – Endurance

"You can't be too high when you win, you can't be too low when you lose. You've got to move on to the next thing."
–Tom Crean

You may get discouraged with your new business ventures or projects, but don't forget to focus on the big picture. Remember that many of the most successful people in the world had very small beginnings and had to work hard for years before they achieved a high level of success. If you are pursuing a project you are truly passionate about, keep going! Think of Winston Churchill's famous advice: "If you're going through hell, keep going."

You don't have to make your microbusiness a full-time job, or even a part-time job, right away. It can be something you work on for a few hours every week for years until you make it a priority, if you ever decide that is the right path for you.

Notice all of the businesses, celebrities, individuals, athletes, blogs, websites, and YouTube videos that have gone viral and gained so much acclaim. Chances are, they all have a few things in common. Learn how they achieved success and take action based on their positive advice and examples. Keep in mind their humble beginnings. Again, so many of the most popular products, services, and people had a very small start. Here are a few examples:

- Coca Cola had an unassuming beginning. In the first year, only 9 glasses of Coca Cola were sold a day![1]
- Apple Computer was rejected for acquisition by Hewlett-Packard and Atari.[2]
- Founders of Google, Larry Page and Sergey Brin, decided to sell Google and focus on school. They offered to sell Google to Excite CEO George Bell for $1 million. He declined, and they decided to keep the company. Today Google is worth more than $250 billion.[3]
- "Howard Schultz grew up in the Brooklyn projects before becoming CEO of Starbucks."[4]
- "Oprah Winfrey turned a life of hardship into inspiration for a multi-billion-dollar empire."[5]

Luckily, all of these people decided to endure their setbacks and move forward!

Earning enough to provide the basics for your family is a great goal in my book, but I also believe that there is nothing wrong with having more ambition. Regardless, goals are different for everybody. The key is to know your goals – you need to have a target.

If you do have ambitious goals, take the advice of Gary Vaynerchuk – "You have to think about building your brand in terms of a marathon, not a sprint."[6] I ran the Chicago Marathon, and I'm currently training for my next one. My goal is to finish the Boston Marathon within the next few years. The race itself requires a lot of patience, but the training requires even more. This kind of endurance applies to many goals – give your projects a chance to grow over time if you truly believe in them.

If something clearly isn't working for you or you aren't enjoying your line of work, then it may be time to move on to another endeavor. A great book to read about the positive side of quitting is called *The Dip* by Seth Godin. Visit Seth at sethgodin.com to check out more of his valuable books and free resources.

Hang in there, and remember that many of the most successful people in the world started small and experienced hardship at some point in their lives.

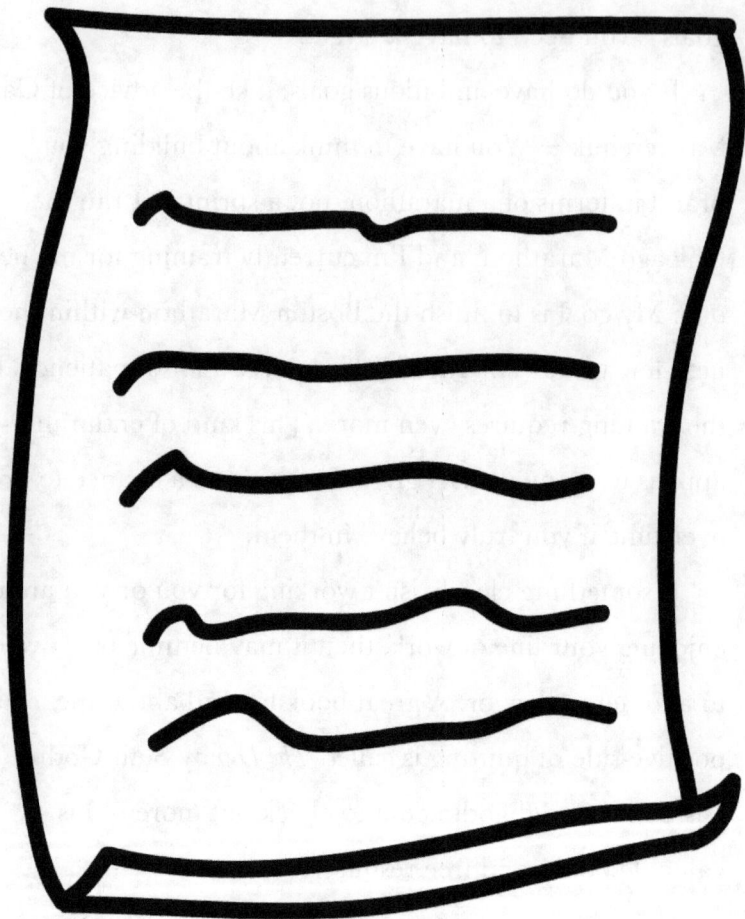

Chapter 10 – Too Much Information

"A wealth of information creates a poverty of attention."
–Herbert A. Simon

Staying informed will be one of your most important tasks as a microbusiness owner. Keeping up-to-date with the most popular products and technologies can serve you well. Why? You can buy these popular products at wholesale prices in bulk online and resell them at retail prices. Many times, you will even be able to compete with retailers by offering lower prices, resulting in a higher volume of sales. Staying informed also helps you be aware of trends. If 'retro' is starting to trend again, you can start to sell some retro items in your store; it's pretty simple.

Alltop.com is one of my favorite places to stay informed. Alltop, Twitter, and an RSS reader are some of the resources I use most frequently for condensing news. There are a variety of news aggregators, so choose one that works for you. My Uncle Chris suggests the apps 'Taptu' and 'Flipboard.' When you search for a topic, all of these tools take you to that category and display stories from relevant news sources. This enables you to see all of the top stories from the most legitimate sources online, all on one page, for any given topic! This also allows you to check for consistency among popular stories while finding other articles more quickly.

The goal is to condense your information intake while keeping up with what's going on in the world. Timothy Ferris, author of several bestsellers, says he doesn't even read the news.[1] If this approach resonates with you, check out his chapter "The Low-Information Diet" in *The 4-Hour Workweek*. For more ideas from Timothy Ferris, read his other releases *The 4-Hour Body* and *The 4-Hour Chef*.

Keeping up with the news has helped me very much with my businesses over the past few years. I go over breaking news and then prioritize the rest of the news I will read. For example, if you're passionate about business, make business news your priority after quickly learning about the top stories. Also be sure to limit your time spent on those top stories...they can waste your day! The same holds true for YouTube videos and TV.

A lunch break and a few five to ten minute breaks will help refresh you during the day. Watching TED Talks and reading random news is fine during those breaks. Most of us have lost track of time, resulting in last minute performances with our work at some point. Condensing our news intake and keeping an eye on our time is a positive habit and solution.

I like to check the news and do research on a variety of other websites. I discover new business blogs by browsing different categories on WordPress and Google Blog Search, and I frequently use *Wikipedia* for research. Some other news sources and aggregators I check include *The Wall Street Journal*, *The Week*, *Mashable*, *The Huffington Post*, *Google News*, *Fast Company*, *Forbes*, and *Yahoo*. These sites are good resources, but some have pop-ups and try to get you to share what you're reading with Facebook. As I discussed in Chapter 5, I make a point to see the positive trends through the sea of bad news.

Back towards the end of 2011, Mark Zuckerberg's Forbes profile said, "What the CIA failed to do in 60 years, Zuck has done in 7: knowing what 800 million people – more than 10% of the world's population – think, read and listen to, plus who they know, what they like and where they live, travel, vote, shop, worship." That number has only increased. Obviously Mr. Zuckerberg has incredible access to information. I'm sure it's not very hard for him to keep up with the latest products and trends; however, the rest of us should continue to condense our information intake while quickly checking the top stories from a variety of sources.

Chapter 11
Anti-Mediocre Marketing Militia

"Products that are remarkable get talked about."

–Seth Godin

....

Trust is Your #1 Resource

You can usually only sell average products for a very limited time. Exceptional products and services coupled with further great marketing is the goal. This approach will also earn you respect.

Remarkable businesses develop a positive reputation and gain trust. This trust is your #1 resource; it is the foundation of your marketing efforts. How do you go about gaining this trust? Here are a few points to consider:

1. Make improving your customers' lives your #1 priority.
2. Be honest. Admit your mistakes and fix them to the best of your ability, but also be sure to acknowledge your achievements.
3. Don't use key ideas from employees, customers, family members, and friends without giving them some kind of recognition and credit.

4. Develop an outstanding sense of perspective – see your products and services from multiple perspectives. Empathize with your customers and employees, and ask yourself if you would be happy with your business if roles were reversed.

5. Be straightforward with your marketing and discard manipulative maneuvers. In this age of information, many of us are catching on to these phony approaches. Be yourself and say what you do with no BS.

6. Be aware that most people are annoyed with spam. Don't email, call, or text anyone too much unless they indicate they want this kind of contact.

7. Be direct with your employees. It's important to treat them with respect and pay them fairly for their efforts.

8. Offer fair prices and be nice to your customers and employees.

9. Don't lie to your competitors. If you don't want them to know confidential information, simply refuse to tell them or anyone else.

10. Offer frequent customers special discounts.

11. Offer anonymous satisfaction reviews to your customers and employees. Be sure to read the

feedback regularly and carefully.

12. Have fun! If you're not, it will be obvious to those around you and discourage confidence.

These are just a few ways to gain trust in your industry. I believe these tactics will help inspire a sterling reputation, which will help you create a remarkable business and gain respect.

Choose a Great Title That Grabs Attention!

"Every time you write, you have an opportunity to communicate and to convince."[1]

–David Meerman Scott

When choosing an advertisement to describe products and services, David Meerman Scott suggests we avoid phrases that are overused.

Overused phrases that are popular in the tech world include *innovative, cutting-edge,* as well as *new and improved.* Using these words in titles decreases our chances of convincing an audience that our products are useful, or our descriptions are authentic, because these terms have become so generic from overuse.

There are definitely exceptions to this rule. I tend to use many of these phrases frequently, but I still think it's an interesting perspective. I'm just doing my best to "bring my 'A' game." Seth Godin also discusses this in his *Encyclopedia of Business Clichés*.[2]

Guerrilla Marketing!

I first read *Guerrilla Marketing* by Jay Conrad Levinson back in 2007. At the time, I had just started a band with some college friends, and I was looking for books to help us promote our music and schedule shows. After reading *Guerrilla Marketing*, I picked up a book by Bob Baker called the *Guerrilla Music Marketing Handbook*. This is the book I referenced the most when it came to music related projects; it's right on target for goal-oriented musicians. My wife and I were fortunate enough to meet Bob in the winter of 2012. He was very uplifting, supportive, and encouraged me to finish this book! Visit Bob at bob-baker.com.

The *Guerrilla Music Marketing Handbook* helped me schedule around 100 concerts in a little over a year when I was playing drums in a rock band during college. We played shows all over Indiana; Chicago, Illinois; Nashville, Tennessee; and Louisville, Kentucky. We were booked every weekend and we even made a small profit – something that has become more difficult for many musicians. My college band was just like a microbusiness venture. I transferred my knowledge of music marketing to microbusiness marketing, which helped me quickly secure work in the beginning phases of my business projects.

As a microbusiness owner, you will spend a great deal of time marketing, promoting, and advertising your products and services. What's the difference between the three? Here's my interpretation:

- <u>Marketing</u> – 100% of your interactions with your customers and potential customers (advertising and promoting are subcategories of marketing). That doesn't mean you're constantly pushing your products and services on everybody. It simply means every interaction you have with people and every aspect of your business is marketing at work. You're continuously developing your reputation even if you're not thinking about it.

- <u>Promoting</u> – Any activity that spreads the word about your products and services. Some of these activities include phone calls, texting, emailing, passing out your business cards, attending business conferences, and talking with people in person and on the internet about what you do.

- <u>Advertising</u>- Communicating with your customers or potential customers through a variety of platforms. These communications inform people about what you do. Popular places to advertise your business include online classifieds, Google, YouTube, social media websites, websites your target audience visits, apps for smart phones and tablets, blogs, the radio, TV, the paper, billboards, and more.

I believe marketing is an ongoing task. Putting ads up online and doing a poor job when you get work is horrible marketing. That's why improving your customers' lives needs to be your main objective.

I do my best to spend at least one hour on my advertisements each day. Many businesses require that you spend the majority of your time on advertising and promotion, but it really depends on what kind of business you're pursuing. When you own a fairly popular website or smart phone app, advertising and promoting usually require more time and become full-time jobs; hiring one or more people to help you with this task may be a good idea if you find yourself in a similar situation.

I'm growing my businesses at my own pace, and I'm really enjoying it. If I began with startup capital and rushed the growth of my business, I may have missed some important steps and had to pay the consequences. Since instead I have stayed small and busy with work, I've been able to learn how to properly move forward rather than skipping critical steps and rushing the learning process.

To help get you started on the path to successfully building your brand, here are some key points from *Guerrilla Marketing* by Jay Conrad Levinson:

- "Marketing is every bit of contact you have with anyone in the outside world."[3]
- "Guerrilla's adapt their marketing, creative message, and entire philosophy to the realities of the times."[4]
- "Don't dive into marketing your name until you've checked that it's available, legal, and protectable."[5]
- "Guerrilla marketing does sell products and services. But it sells them only once. It's the high quality you offer that will bring in the repeat and referral sales."[6]

The Power of Search Engine Optimization

When you have a question, what's the first thing you do? Many of us use a search engine to find a quick answer as the first step in the research process.

Recently, it's been difficult to avoid information about search engine optimization (SEO). Every time you use Google, Yahoo, Bing, or any other web search engine to answer one of your questions, SEO is hard at work. "SEO is the process of affecting the visibility of a website or a web page in a search engine's "natural" or un-paid ("organic") search results."[7] Having great SEO for your products and services is crucial for sales.

When you need a product or service, do you search for potential solutions on Google and compare prices, or do you wait for an annoying salesperson to call or email you? I personally always research using search engines and most of the people I know do the same.

Keep track of how social media connects to SEO. Social media sites can help strengthen your SEO – when you share your links on Twitter, Facebook, Google+, and LinkedIn, it helps the ranking of your website. The more people who reshare or retweet your links, the more relevant your site or blog will be in search results. If you haven't chosen a name for your business, make sure the domain name is available. This will increase the chances of your business name showing up on the first page when somebody looks for your business with a search engine. The solution to a person's problem may even be in your domain name, which will be a victory for your SEO. Imagine owning dictionary.com. I always use Go Daddy for my domain purchases, but many people use other sites – find one that works best for you.

The number of people you can reach with SEO each week is so much greater than the few hundred you can reach with 3-4 people making phone calls. Here's the catch: you only need a small team of people who are experts at SEO and social media to reach an incredible amount of individuals.

Solution: Hire sales people who are also adept at SEO. Give SEO just as much, if not more, attention than sales calls and emails. Building a strong SEO team for your company is vital.

Where do you go if you want to subcontract your SEO work? There are many people out there who charge way too much to help you with SEO; you should be very selective if you choose to hire someone to help you. Reading a variety of books about the topic will be a great way to get familiar with it if you aren't already. Be sure to hire a reputable company with a track record of good results if you decide you need more help.

Search engine optimization is still young. In the year 2000 it wasn't nearly as important as it is today. SEO is only going to become more important and the process is constantly evolving; staying cognizant of its changes is critical.

Remember: SEO, advertising, and promoting are secondary to exceptional products and services that improve your customers' lives.

Chapter 12 – Keeping Your Sense of Humor

"A joke is a very serious thing."

–Winston Churchill

As you know, keeping your sense of humor is one of the most important things you can do. I often spend my spare time with my wife and friends watching comedy TV shows, funny YouTube videos, and attending a place in my town that hosts stand-up comedians called *The Comedy Attic*.

Life is too short to be serious or humorous all of the time – here, as with most things, a good balance is ideal. There have been business meetings that did not go well for me because I was too serious or too comedic. Now, when speaking with customers, I make it clear that I'm taking their time seriously and want to give them value for their money. Certain customers are great to joke with, though. You have to judge each interaction individually and decide what tone is appropriate.

When I get a job done, I have some free time to watch *South Park*, read reddit, and watch funny YouTube videos. For more life advice, listen to "YOLO" by The Lonely Island.[1] Though the song is obviously meant to be funny and a dig at people giving too much advice, Kendrick Lamar is right when he recommends freelancing!

If you think *South Park* is ridiculous, watch more episodes. It has been an educational and funny show for me since I was in 3rd or 4th grade – the same grade the boys are in on the show. I even did a project on it in a senior-level college course while studying at Indiana University.

Trey Parker and Matt Stone have a bizarre talent for being remarkably accurate with their portrayal of the world through the characters in *South Park*, which makes it even more hysterical.

Watch, read, and listen to media you find humorous on a weekly basis. It makes life more enjoyable.

Here are some shows, aside from *South Park*, that I enjoy:

- *Saturday Night Live* –Way to ship!
- *Futurama*
- *30 Rock*
- *Tosh.0*
- *American Dad*
- *Arrested Development*
- *Parks and Recreation* – Check out the Swanson Pyramid of Greatness.[2]
- *Raising Hope* – Burt is a microbusiness owner!

I'm not going to include the long list of my favorite comedy movies, but here are a few:

- *Ted*
- *The Hangover*
- *The Big Lebowski*
- *Anchorman*
- *Ghostbusters*
- *Toy Story 1-3*
- *Little Miss Sunshine*
- *Caddy Shack*
- *Paul*
- *Get Him to the Greek*
- *Hot Tub Time Machine*
- *Zombieland*
- *This is 40*

The list goes on! I'm constantly looking for new comedy releases.

Chapter 13 – Give it Away Now

A simple gift given to Anthony Kiedis, the lead singer of the Red Hot Chili Peppers, inspired one of my favorite songs, "Give It Away."

Nina Hagen gave Kiedis the nicest jacket in her closet after he commented on how cool it was. She explained, "It's always important to give things away; it creates good energy. If you have a closet full of clothes, and you try to keep them all, your life will get very small. But if you have a full closet and someone sees something they like, if you give it to them, the world is a better place."[1]

This brings us to an important point: You can make your microbusiness a charity if you have a good full-time job or already have another successful business. The profits from your microbusiness can go to a positive cause you support or your business can benefit others directly. I know a studio engineer who offers free recording time to musicians who can't afford to record in traditional studios. He has a good job and wants to give back to other musicians around him. You're a good man, John.

We often hear about the importance of giving time and money to charities, organizations, and people we support. I've heard and read the opinion that many people give just to feel better about themselves and that there are no people who are truly altruistic. I disagree with that standpoint.

I've experienced gifts from people who gave to truly make a positive impact on my life. My friends and I have also shared time and money with organizations to simply help. No, we didn't do it to strictly feel good about ourselves and tell everyone about our contributions afterwards.

Give simply to help, don't expect anything in return, and forget about it. If you are giving just to create good karma for yourself, you are missing the point. You should be giving to create a positive experience for the people and organizations around you – end of story.

After you save at least 10% of your own money, give away at least another 5 – 10% of the money you have earned. By purchasing this book, you have helped give to charity: water, a non-profit organization bringing safe, clean drinking water to developing countries. Visit them at charitywater.org for more information about their admirable cause.

If you are earning zero dollars or can't afford to give any money away, you still probably have a few hours of time on your hands each week. Go help clean up your town or volunteer your time to one of the many organizations that would love your help.

The Me Monster!

Beware of the me monster! It's human nature to be self-centered from time to time. We want to feel good about ourselves, so sometimes we get lost in our own problems. Do your best to give the teams and organizations you support your attention. Instead of tearing others down, build them up. Give the world your time and positive energy. Thank you to comedian Brian Regan for his me monster skit![2]

In the business world, it's important to care about the well-being of others. When a person truly cares about solving your problems, it will show in their actions and body language. They will go the extra mile, and they will make sure they are fair with you. You're more likely to do business with the people who care about you over the people who just care about themselves and the bottom line.

Take Responsibility

I recently watched *The Lorax* and was happy with the message: take responsibility and understand the ramifications of your actions. I admit, it's difficult to truly comprehend every consequence of your actions. But do your best to take actions that benefit yourself, other people, and the world.

Chapter 14 – Happiness & Freedom

I've never been happier since starting my business ventures. Although I worked as a 9-5 employee for a few nice businesses, pursuing my own projects has given me a greater sense of happiness, freedom, and purpose.

You may not have a positive experience with your business ventures, or you may have an amazing time with your projects while experiencing great success. I hope you have an extraordinary time, and I wish I could guarantee your happiness and a favorable outcome.

In his intriguing book *Stumbling on Happiness,* Daniel Gilbert points out happiness can be a complex topic. I recommend reading his book for detailed thoughts on happiness.

You'll likely experience good times and bad times, just like everyone else. Ups and downs are a part of the game. Many other happy employees, business owners, and professionals will share their secrets of happiness and success with you. I've found a lot of them are sincerely doing their best to help others and make this world a better place. Sometimes their advice will really connect with you and make your life better.

What will you do with all of this advice? Your dad may believe being an engineer is the ticket to happiness while another good friend will tell you being a doctor is the way to go. I loved listening to different perspectives as a kid and I still do. Many people went out of their way to share with me what worked for them. Now I'm sharing what is working for me. I wish you well and hope this book helps you with your life and businesses! Go launch a brighter future!

I did my best to keep this book short. It was originally going to be single-spaced and 200 pages. I realized this did not match an underlying theme of the book: a micro approach can be more effective than making projects bigger and more complex than they need to be. The same ideas that were in the longer version are in this condensed, better version. I hope you've enjoyed this microbook!

Stay Connected!

AnthonyHilb.com
MicrobusinessOwners.com – visit the launch pad for free resources!

Facebook.com/anthonyhilb
Facebook.com/microbizowners
@anthonyhilb
@microbizowners

anthonyhilb@gmail.com
microbusinessowners@gmail.com

About

Since I started life with a very rough beginning, I know exactly how it feels to struggle and lose hope. Yet I believe having a hopeful mindset is the beginning to a better future. When I was losing hope and felt like dying as a starving five year old, I vividly remember asking myself, "Is this how life is always going to be?"

Asking myself this most important question kept me going; it gave me hope that maybe I could have a better life one day. To my surprise, I was taken away from my biological mother and family as a child. It was sad, but it was also the luckiest thing that ever happened to me. I'm infinitely grateful to the Hilb family for taking me in.

This same kind of hope is necessary for a multitude of situations. I experienced a similar kind of hopeless feeling as I did when I was a child (though on a much lesser scale) when I entered the job market after college in 2010. At the time, I didn't have my life together, and I was uninspired. This led to searching for any kind of inspiration, which helped me find inspirational books about business.

After experiencing a few traditional jobs, I changed my plans and began to apply what I learned from all of the business books I picked up.

Fortunately, I found work within a week and have continued to stay busy with my microbusinesses every single week since I've started.

Although I've only owned microbusinesses for a few years, I realized the abundance of microbusiness work opportunities that will be available for many years to come. This gave me a sense of urgency to release this book. It's my goal to help anyone confused about working and earning money.

I panicked when I thought I was doomed to work low paid employee positions or in boring offices for the rest of my life after college. Luckily, I discovered this is far from the truth. Certain things in life are out of our control, but other situations can be controlled by our actions. Becoming a business owner has taught me that it's very possible to make a living on your own terms with hard work and a little bit of luck. It also taught me that I can help people and give them fair deals while also making just as much and often times even more than I would working for someone else at a traditional job.

If you're searching for inspiration, it's my hope that this book will help you. Everybody is different, and you obviously don't have to be a business owner to benefit from reading business related topics. Over the years, I've recognized that inspiration comes from all walks of life. From the teacher, musician, athlete, artist, business owner, doctor, lawyer, office worker, physical laborer, mother, to the talented scientist, everyone has something to share. If you take the time to see things from their perspective, you will probably learn something very useful and be inspired.

References

Chapter 0

1. *Guide to size standards.* Retrieved from http://www.sba.gov/content/guide-size-standards
2. *Definition of microbusiness.* Retrieved from http://oxforddictionaries.com/definition/english/microbusiness?q=microbusiness
3. Brown, C. (2013, February 01). *Marketing wizard seth godin on success and inspiration.* Retrieved from http://www.entrepreneur.com/article/225447
4. Segall, L. (2012, April 09). *Facebook acquires instagram for $1 billion.* Retrieved from http://money.cnn.com/2012/04/09/technology/facebook_acquires_instagram/
5. *Defining micro business.* (n.d.). Retrieved from http://microbusiness.vistaprint.com/wp-content/uploads/2011/03/define-micro-business.jpg
6. Lynley, M. (2013, February 03). 'minecraft' hits mother lode for a small swedish company. *The Wall Street Journal.* Retrieved from http://online.wsj.com/article/SB10001424127887323807004578282142065371984.html?mod=e2tw

7. Fried, J., & Heinemeier Hansson, D. (2010). *Rework*. (p. 23). New York, New York: Crown Publishing.

8. Gates, B. (1999). *Business @ the speed of thought*. (p. 262). New York, New York: Warner Books.

9. http://www.youtube.com/watch?v=UuHILqDIvis Retrieved September 20, 2012

Chapter 1

1. Foreman, G. (2002). George foreman's guide to life. (p. 118). New York, NY: Simon & Schuster

2. Branson, R. (2008). Business stripped bare. (pp. 13-19). New York, NY: Virgin Books.

3. Branson, R. (2008). Business stripped bare. (p. 33). New York, NY: Virgin Books.

4. Branson, R. (2008). Business stripped bare. (p. 10). New York, NY: Virgin Books.

Chapter 2

1. Guillebeau, C. (2012). *The $100 startup*. (p. XVI). New York, NY: Crown Publishing

Chapter 3

1. Fried, J., & Heinemeier Hansson, D. (2010). Rework. (p. 121). New York, New York: Crown Publishing.

2. Trex, E. (n.d.). *7 wildly successful people who survived bankruptcy*. Retrieved from http://blogs.static.mentalfloss.com/blogs/archives/203 36.html

3. Kirkpatrick, D. (2010). *The facebook effect*. (pp. 30-35). New York, NY: Simon & Schuster.

4. Kirkpatrick, D. (2010). *The facebook effect*. (p. 86). New York, NY: Simon & Schuster.

5. Kirkpatrick, D. (2010). *The facebook effect*. (p. 63). New York, NY: Simon & Schuster.

6. Kirkpatrick, D. (2010). *The facebook effect*. (p. 89). New York, NY: Simon & Schuster.

Chapter 4

1. Mackay, H. (2011). *The mackay mba of selling in the real world*. (p. 58). New York, NY: Penguin.

2. Dennis, F. (2010). *The narrow road*. (p. 19). New York, NY: Penguin.

Chapter 5

1. Diamandis, P., & Kotler, S. (2012). *Abundance.* New York, NY: Free Press.
2. Diamandis, P., & Kotler, S. (2012). *Abundance.* (p. 148). New York, NY: Free Press.
3. Diamandis, P., & Kotler, S. (2012). *Abundance.* (p. 10). New York, NY: Free Press.
4. Diamandis, P., & Kotler, S. (2012). *Abundance.* (p. 26). New York, NY: Free Press.
5. Diamandis, P., & Kotler, S. (2012). *Abundance.* (p. 6). New York, NY: Free Press.
6. Diamandis, P., & Kotler, S. (2012). *Abundance.* (p. 229). New York, NY: Free Press.

Chapter 6

1. (2010). *Start your own business.* (p. 155). Entrepreneur Press.
2. The picture I posted on reddit. (Helping my friend make scrapple for dinner) http://imgur.com/a/XJCZK
3. Cuban, Mark (2011-11-19). *How to Win at the Sport of Business: If I Can Do It, You Can Do It* (Kindle Locations 585-586). Diversion Books. Kindle Edition.

4. Cuban, Mark (2011-11-19*). How to Win at the Sport of Business: If I Can Do It, You Can Do It* (Kindle Location 587). Diversion Books. Kindle Edition.

5. *27 microbusiness tools you didn't know you needed.* (2013, January 24). Retrieved from http://smallbusiness.uprinting.com/27-essential-microbusiness-tools-you-should-try-out/

6. *30 best sites to find freelance jobs.* (2012, February 20). Retrieved from http://www.tripwiremagazine.com/2012/02/freelancer-jobs.html

Chapter 7

1. Hinshaw, M. (2012, April 24). *Instagram vs. kodak: Smart customers sidestep stupid companies.* Retrieved from http://www.huffingtonpost.com/michael-hinshaw/instagram-vs-kodak-smart-_b_1448917.html

2. Dennis, F. (2010). *The narrow road.* (p. 19). New York, NY: Penguin.

Chapter 9

1. *The coca cola company heritage timeline.* (n.d.). Retrieved from http://heritage.coca-cola.com/
2. Mackay, H. (2011). *The mackay mba of selling in the real world.* (p. 96). New York, NY: Penguin.
3. Siegler, M. (2010, September 29). *When google wanted to sell to excite for under $1 million — and they passed.* Retrieved from http://techcrunch.com/2010/09/29/google-excite/
4. Nisen, M. (2012, December 28). *20 inspiring rags-to-riches stories.* Retrieved from http://finance.yahoo.com/news/20-inspiring-rags-to-riches-stories-181933596.html?page=all
5. Nisen, M. (2012, December 28). *20 inspiring rags-to-riches stories.* Retrieved from http://finance.yahoo.com/news/20-inspiring-rags-to-riches-stories-181933596.html?page=all
6. Vaynerchuk, G. (2009). *Crush it!.* (p. 93). New York, NY: HarperCollins.

Chapter 10

1. Ferriss, T. (2009). *The 4-hour workweek.* (p. 86). New York, NY: Crown Publishing.

Chapter 11

1. Meerman Scott, D. (2011). *The new rules of marketing and pr*. (p. 185). Hoboken, NJ: John Wiley & Sons.

2. Godin, S. (2007, August 14). *The encyclopedia of business cliches*. Retrieved from http://www.squidoo.com/businesscliches

3. Conrad Levinson, J. (2007). *Guerrilla marketing*. (p. 3). New York, NY: Houghton Mifflin Company.

4. Conrad Levinson, J. (2007). *Guerrilla marketing*. (p. 57). New York, NY: Houghton Mifflin Company.

5.   Conrad Levinson, J. (2007). *Guerrilla marketing*. (p. 309). New York, NY: Houghton Mifflin Company.

6. Conrad Levinson, J. (2007). *Guerrilla marketing*. (p. 313). New York, NY: Houghton Mifflin Company.

7. Wikipedia. (n.d.). *Search engine optimization*. Retrieved from http://en.wikipedia.org/wiki/Search_engine_optimization

Chapter 12

1. "Yolo" by The Lonely Island (n.d.). Retrieved from http://www.youtube.com/watch?v=z5Otla5157c
2. *Swanson pyramid of greatness.* (n.d.). Retrieved from http://img2.timeinc.net/ew/dynamic/imgs/110120/park -recs-pyramid_1500.jpg

Chapter 13

1. Kiedis, A., & Sloman, L. (2004). *Scar tissue.* (p. 273). New York, NY: Hyperion.
2. Regan, B. (n.d.). *The me monster.* Retrieved from http://www.youtube.com/watch?v=fVWHa5cpMZo

www.ingramcontent.com/pod-product-compliance
Lightning Source LLC
LaVergne TN
LVHW021508080426
835509LV00018B/2443